This journal belongs to:

How to use this journal

The Reading Log journal is designed to help you keep track of your reading journey in a simple and organised way. A place to reflect on your current reads and helping you to plan what to choose next.

Use the 'Reading Log' section to list all the books that you've read. Whenever you finish a book, jot down its title and your rating of it. There is space to write down a short summary, your thoughts, favourite quotes, memorable characters, and any reflections you have on the book as a whole. This section allows you to capture your impressions while they're fresh in your mind.

Then you can add the page number of your book review to the reading log for easy future referencing.

In the 'Books To Read' section, make a list of all the titles you want to read in the future. By using this journal regularly, you'll not only keep track of your reading progress but also create a personal record of your literary journey.

Index

Reading Log

Reading Log . . .

Date	Title	Rating	Page

Date	Title	Rating	Page

Reading Log . . .

Date	Title	Rating	Page

Date	Title	Rating	Page

Book Reviews

My Review . . .

Title: ....

Author: ....

Date: .... Rating: ☆☆☆☆☆

☐ Book   ☐ Audiobook   ☐ eBook

I would recommend this book to:

....

Summary

....
....
....
....
....
....
....
....
....

Best Characters & Why I Liked Them

....
....
....
....

My Thoughts

_____
_____
_____
_____
_____
_____
_____
_____
_____
_____
_____

Best Quotes & Stand Out Moments

	Page

My Review . . .

Title: ....

Author: ....

Date: .... Rating: ☆☆☆☆☆

☐ Book   ☐ Audiobook   ☐ eBook

I would recommend this book to:

....

Summary

....

....

....

....

....

....

....

....

....

Best Characters & Why I Liked Them

....

....

....

....

My Thoughts

Best Quotes & Stand Out Moments

Page

My Review . . .

Title: ....

Author: ....

Date: .... Rating: ☆ ☆ ☆ ☆ ☆

☐ Book ☐ Audiobook ☐ eBook

I would recommend this book to:

....

Summary

....

....

....

....

....

....

....

....

....

Best Characters & Why I Liked Them

....

....

....

....

My Thoughts

....
....
....
....
....
....
....
....
....
....
....

Best Quotes & Stand Out Moments

	Page

My Review . . .

Title: ....

Author: ....

Date: .... Rating: ☆☆☆☆☆

☐ Book　☐ Audiobook　☐ eBook

I would recommend this book to:

....

Summary

....
....
....
....
....
....
....
....
....
....

Best Characters & Why I Liked Them

....
....
....
....

My Thoughts

....
....
....
....
....
....
....
....
....
....
....

Best Quotes & Stand Out Moments

	Page

My Review . . .

Title:..

Author:..

Date:................................ Rating: ☆☆☆☆☆

☐ Book ☐ Audiobook ☐ eBook

I would recommend this book to:

....

Summary

....
....
....
....
....
....
....
....
....
....

Best Characters & Why I Liked Them

....
....
....
....

My Thoughts

....
....
....
....
....
....
....
....
....
....
....
....

Best Quotes & Stand Out Moments

	Page

My Review . . .

Title: ....

Author: ....

Date: .... Rating: ☆☆☆☆☆

☐ Book ☐ Audiobook ☐ eBook

I would recommend this book to:

....

Summary

....
....
....
....
....
....
....
....
....
....
....

Best Characters & Why I Liked Them

....
....
....
....

My Thoughts

Best Quotes & Stand Out Moments

Page

My Review . . .

Title: ....

Author: ....

Date: .... Rating: ☆☆☆☆☆

☐ Book   ☐ Audiobook   ☐ eBook

I would recommend this book to:

....

Summary

....
....
....
....
....
....
....
....
....
....

Best Characters & Why I Liked Them

....
....
....
....

My Thoughts

_____

_____

_____

_____

_____

_____

_____

_____

_____

_____

_____

_____

Best Quotes & Stand Out Moments

	Page

My Review . . .

Title:...

Author:..

Date:... Rating: ☆☆☆☆☆

☐ Book   ☐ Audiobook   ☐ eBook

I would recommend this book to:

....

Summary

....
....
....
....
....
....
....
....
....

Best Characters & Why I Liked Them

....
....
....

My Thoughts

....
....
....
....
....
....
....
....
....
....

Best Quotes & Stand Out Moments

	Page

My Review . . .

Title: ....

Author: ....

Date: .... Rating: ☆☆☆☆☆

☐ Book ☐ Audiobook ☐ eBook

I would recommend this book to:

....

Summary

....
....
....
....
....
....
....
....
....
....

Best Characters & Why I Liked Them

....
....
....
....

My Thoughts

....
....
....
....
....
....
....
....
....
....
....
....

Best Quotes & Stand Out Moments

	Page

My Review . . .

Title: ....

Author: ....

Date: .... Rating: ☆ ☆ ☆ ☆ ☆

☐ Book   ☐ Audiobook   ☐ eBook

I would recommend this book to:

....

Summary

....

....

....

....

....

....

....

....

Best Characters & Why I Liked Them

....

....

....

....

My Thoughts

....
....
....
....
....
....
....
....
....
....

Best Quotes & Stand Out Moments

	Page
....	
....	
....	
....	
....	
....	
....	
....	
....	
....	
....	
....	

My Review . . .

Title: ....

Author: ....

Date: .... Rating: ☆ ☆ ☆ ☆ ☆

☐ Book ☐ Audiobook ☐ eBook

I would recommend this book to:

....

Summary

....

....

....

....

....

....

....

....

....

Best Characters & Why I Liked Them

....

....

....

....

My Thoughts

Best Quotes & Stand Out Moments

Page

My Review . . .

Title: ....

Author: ....

Date: .... Rating: ☆ ☆ ☆ ☆ ☆

☐ Book ☐ Audiobook ☐ eBook

I would recommend this book to:

....

Summary

....
....
....
....
....
....
....
....
....
....

Best Characters & Why I Liked Them

....
....
....
....

My Thoughts

....

....

....

....

....

....

....

....

....

....

....

Best Quotes & Stand Out Moments

	Page

My Review . . .

Title:..

Author:..

Date:...................................... Rating: ☆☆☆☆☆

☐ Book ☐ Audiobook ☐ eBook

I would recommend this book to:

....

Summary

....
....
....
....
....
....
....
....
....

Best Characters & Why I Liked Them

....
....
....
....

My Thoughts

_____
_____
_____
_____
_____
_____
_____
_____
_____
_____
_____

Best Quotes & Stand Out Moments

	Page

My Review . . .

Title: ....

Author: ....

Date: .... Rating: ☆☆☆☆☆

☐ Book ☐ Audiobook ☐ eBook

I would recommend this book to:

....

Summary

....

....

....

....

....

....

....

....

....

Best Characters & Why I Liked Them

....

....

....

....

My Thoughts

....
....
....
....
....
....
....
....
....
....
....
....

Best Quotes & Stand Out Moments

	Page

My Review . . .

Title: ....

Author: ....

Date: .... Rating: ☆ ☆ ☆ ☆ ☆

☐ Book ☐ Audiobook ☐ eBook

I would recommend this book to:

....

Summary

....
....
....
....
....
....
....
....
....
....

Best Characters & Why I Liked Them

....
....
....
....

My Thoughts

....
....
....
....
....
....
....
....
....
....
....
....
....
....

Best Quotes & Stand Out Moments

	Page
....	
....	
....	
....	
....	
....	
....	
....	
....	
....	
....	

My Review...

Title:...

Author:...

Date:.................................. Rating: ☆☆☆☆☆

☐ Book   ☐ Audiobook   ☐ eBook

I would recommend this book to:

....

Summary

....
....
....
....
....
....
....
....
....

Best Characters & Why I Liked Them

....
....
....
....

My Thoughts

Best Quotes & Stand Out Moments

Page

My Review . . .

Title:...

Author:..

Date:.. Rating: ☆☆☆☆☆

☐ Book ☐ Audiobook ☐ eBook

I would recommend this book to:

....

Summary

....
....
....
....
....
....
....
....
....
....

Best Characters & Why I Liked Them

....
....
....
....

My Thoughts

....
....
....
....
....
....
....
....
....
....
....

Best Quotes & Stand Out Moments

	Page

My Review . . .

Title:...

Author:..

Date:.. Rating: ☆☆☆☆☆

☐ Book   ☐ Audiobook   ☐ eBook

I would recommend this book to:

....

Summary

....
....
....
....
....
....
....
....
....
....

Best Characters & Why I Liked Them

....
....
....
....

My Thoughts

Best Quotes & Stand Out Moments

Page

My Review . . .

Title: ....

Author: ....

Date: .... Rating: ☆☆☆☆☆

☐ Book ☐ Audiobook ☐ eBook

I would recommend this book to:

....

Summary

....
....
....
....
....
....
....
....
....
....

Best Characters & Why I Liked Them

....
....
....
....

My Thoughts

Best Quotes & Stand Out Moments

	Page

My Review . . .

Title:...

Author:...

Date:................................. Rating: ☆☆☆☆☆

☐ Book ☐ Audiobook ☐ eBook

I would recommend this book to:

....

Summary

....
....
....
....
....
....
....
....
....
....

Best Characters & Why I Liked Them

....
....
....
....

My Thoughts

Best Quotes & Stand Out Moments

	Page

My Review . . .

Title:...

Author:...

Date:.. Rating: ☆☆☆☆☆

☐ Book ☐ Audiobook ☐ eBook

I would recommend this book to:

....

Summary

....
....
....
....
....
....
....
....
....
....

Best Characters & Why I Liked Them

....
....
....
....

My Thoughts

Best Quotes & Stand Out Moments

Page

My Review . . .

Title:...

Author:...

Date:... Rating: ☆☆☆☆☆

☐ Book ☐ Audiobook ☐ eBook

I would recommend this book to:

....

Summary

....

....

....

....

....

....

....

....

....

Best Characters & Why I Liked Them

....

....

....

....

My Thoughts

Best Quotes & Stand Out Moments

Page

My Review . . .

Title: ....

Author: ....

Date: .... Rating: ☆☆☆☆☆

☐ Book ☐ Audiobook ☐ eBook

I would recommend this book to:

....

Summary

....

....

....

....

....

....

....

....

....

Best Characters & Why I Liked Them

....

....

....

....

My Thoughts

....
....
....
....
....
....
....
....
....
....

Best Quotes & Stand Out Moments

	Page

....
....
....
....
....
....
....
....
....
....
....
....
....

My Review . . .

Title: ....

Author: ....

Date: .... Rating: ☆☆☆☆☆

☐ Book ☐ Audiobook ☐ eBook

I would recommend this book to:

....

Summary

....
....
....
....
....
....
....
....
....

Best Characters & Why I Liked Them

....
....
....
....

My Thoughts

....
....
....
....
....
....
....
....
....
....
....

Best Quotes & Stand Out Moments

	Page

My Review . . .

Title:...

Author:...

Date:... Rating: ☆ ☆ ☆ ☆ ☆

☐ Book   ☐ Audiobook   ☐ eBook

I would recommend this book to:

....

Summary

....
....
....
....
....
....
....
....
....
....

Best Characters & Why I Liked Them

....
....
....
....

My Thoughts

....

....

....

....

....

....

....

....

....

....

Best Quotes & Stand Out Moments

	Page

My Review . . .

Title:..

Author:..

Date:..................................... Rating: ☆☆☆☆☆

☐ Book ☐ Audiobook ☐ eBook

I would recommend this book to:

....

Summary

....
....
....
....
....
....
....
....
....

Best Characters & Why I Liked Them

....
....
....
....

My Thoughts

....

....

....

....

....

....

....

....

....

....

....

Best Quotes & Stand Out Moments

	Page

My Review . . .

Title: ....

Author: ....

Date: .... Rating: ☆☆☆☆☆

☐ Book ☐ Audiobook ☐ eBook

I would recommend this book to:

....

Summary

....
....
....
....
....
....
....
....
....
....

Best Characters & Why I Liked Them

....
....
....
....

My Thoughts

Best Quotes & Stand Out Moments

	Page

My Review . . .

Title: ....

Author: ....

Date: .... Rating: ☆ ☆ ☆ ☆ ☆

☐ Book ☐ Audiobook ☐ eBook

I would recommend this book to:

....

── Summary ──────────────────────

....

....

....

....

....

....

....

....

── Best Characters & Why I Liked Them ──────

....

....

....

....

My Thoughts

Best Quotes & Stand Out Moments

Page

My Review . . .

Title: ....

Author: ....

Date: .... Rating: ☆☆☆☆☆

☐ Book ☐ Audiobook ☐ eBook

I would recommend this book to:

....

Summary

....

....

....

....

....

....

....

....

....

....

Best Characters & Why I Liked Them

....

....

....

....

My Thoughts

Best Quotes & Stand Out Moments

Page

My Review . . .

Title: ....

Author: ....

Date: .... Rating: ☆ ☆ ☆ ☆ ☆

☐ Book ☐ Audiobook ☐ eBook

I would recommend this book to:

....

Summary

....
....
....
....
....
....
....
....
....

Best Characters & Why I Liked Them

....
....
....
....

My Thoughts

....
....
....
....
....
....
....
....
....
....
....

Best Quotes & Stand Out Moments

Page

....
....
....
....
....
....
....
....
....
....
....
....

My Review . . .

Title:...

Author:..

Date:.. Rating: ☆☆☆☆☆

☐ Book   ☐ Audiobook   ☐ eBook

I would recommend this book to:

....

Summary

....
....
....
....
....
....
....
....
....

Best Characters & Why I Liked Them

....
....
....

My Thoughts

....
....
....
....
....
....
....
....
....
....

Best Quotes & Stand Out Moments

	Page

My Review . . .

Title: ....

Author: ....

Date: .... Rating: ☆☆☆☆☆

☐ Book   ☐ Audiobook   ☐ eBook

I would recommend this book to:

....

Summary

....
....
....
....
....
....
....
....
....
....
....

Best Characters & Why I Liked Them

....
....
....
....

My Thoughts

Best Quotes & Stand Out Moments

Page

My Review . . .

Title:..

Author:...

Date:... Rating: ☆☆☆☆☆

☐ Book   ☐ Audiobook   ☐ eBook

I would recommend this book to:

....

Summary

....
....
....
....
....
....
....
....
....
....

Best Characters & Why I Liked Them

....
....
....
....

My Thoughts

Best Quotes & Stand Out Moments

Page

My Review . . .

Title:...

Author:...

Date:.. Rating: ☆ ☆ ☆ ☆ ☆

☐ Book   ☐ Audiobook   ☐ eBook

I would recommend this book to:

....

Summary

....
....
....
....
....
....
....
....
....

Best Characters & Why I Liked Them

....
....
....
....

My Thoughts

....
....
....
....
....
....
....
....
....
....

Best Quotes & Stand Out Moments

	Page

My Review . . .

Title: ....

Author: ....

Date: .... Rating: ☆☆☆☆☆

☐ Book ☐ Audiobook ☐ eBook

I would recommend this book to:

....

Summary

....
....
....
....
....
....
....
....
....

Best Characters & Why I Liked Them

....
....
....
....

My Thoughts

....
....
....
....
....
....
....
....
....
....
....

Best Quotes & Stand Out Moments

	Page

My Review . . .

Title:...

Author:...

Date:.. Rating: ☆☆☆☆☆

☐ Book ☐ Audiobook ☐ eBook

I would recommend this book to:

....

Summary

....
....
....
....
....
....
....
....
....
....

Best Characters & Why I Liked Them

....
....
....
....

My Thoughts

_____
_____
_____
_____
_____
_____
_____
_____
_____
_____

Best Quotes & Stand Out Moments

	Page

My Review . . .

Title: ....

Author: ....

Date: .... Rating: ☆☆☆☆☆

☐ Book ☐ Audiobook ☐ eBook

I would recommend this book to:

....

Summary

....
....
....
....
....
....
....
....
....
....

Best Characters & Why I Liked Them

....
....
....
....

My Thoughts

Best Quotes & Stand Out Moments

	Page

My Review . . .

Title: ....

Author: ....

Date: .... Rating: ☆☆☆☆☆

☐ Book ☐ Audiobook ☐ eBook

I would recommend this book to:

. . . .

Summary

. . . .

. . . .

. . . .

. . . .

. . . .

. . . .

. . . .

. . . .

Best Characters & Why I Liked Them

. . . .

. . . .

. . . .

. . . .

My Thoughts

....
....
....
....
....
....
....
....
....
....
....

Best Quotes & Stand Out Moments

	Page

My Review . . .

Title:..

Author:...

Date:... Rating: ☆☆☆☆☆

☐ Book   ☐ Audiobook   ☐ eBook

I would recommend this book to:

....

Summary

....

....

....

....

....

....

....

....

....

Best Characters & Why I Liked Them

....

....

....

....

My Thoughts

Best Quotes & Stand Out Moments

Page

My Review . . .

Title: ....

Author: ....

Date: .... Rating: ☆☆☆☆☆

☐ Book ☐ Audiobook ☐ eBook

I would recommend this book to:

....

Summary

....

....

....

....

....

....

....

....

....

Best Characters & Why I Liked Them

....

....

....

....

My Thoughts

Best Quotes & Stand Out Moments

	Page

My Review . . .

Title: ....

Author: ....

Date: .... Rating: ☆☆☆☆☆

☐ Book ☐ Audiobook ☐ eBook

I would recommend this book to:

....

Summary

....

....

....

....

....

....

....

....

Best Characters & Why I Liked Them

....

....

....

My Thoughts

Best Quotes & Stand Out Moments

	Page

My Review . . .

Title:...

Author:...

Date:.. Rating: ☆ ☆ ☆ ☆ ☆

☐ Book   ☐ Audiobook   ☐ eBook

I would recommend this book to:
....

Summary
....
....
....
....
....
....
....
....
....

Best Characters & Why I Liked Them
....
....
....
....

My Thoughts

Best Quotes & Stand Out Moments

	Page

My Review . . .

Title: ....

Author: ....

Date: .... Rating: ☆ ☆ ☆ ☆ ☆

☐ Book ☐ Audiobook ☐ eBook

I would recommend this book to:

....

Summary

....

....

....

....

....

....

....

....

....

Best Characters & Why I Liked Them

....

....

....

My Thoughts

Best Quotes & Stand Out Moments

Page

My Review . . .

Title: ....

Author: ....

Date: .... Rating: ☆ ☆ ☆ ☆ ☆

☐ Book ☐ Audiobook ☐ eBook

I would recommend this book to:

....

Summary

....

....

....

....

....

....

....

....

....

Best Characters & Why I Liked Them

....

....

....

....

My Thoughts

....
....
....
....
....
....
....
....
....
....
....

Best Quotes & Stand Out Moments

	Page
....	
....	
....	
....	
....	
....	
....	
....	
....	
....	
....	

My Review . . .

Title:..

Author:...

Date:.. Rating: ☆☆☆☆☆

☐ Book ☐ Audiobook ☐ eBook

I would recommend this book to:

....

Summary

....

....

....

....

....

....

....

....

....

Best Characters & Why I Liked Them

....

....

....

....

My Thoughts

....
....
....
....
....
....
....
....
....
....

Best Quotes & Stand Out Moments

Page

....
....
....
....
....
....
....
....
....
....
....

My Review . . .

Title: ....

Author: ....

Date: .... Rating: ☆ ☆ ☆ ☆ ☆

☐ Book ☐ Audiobook ☐ eBook

I would recommend this book to:

....

Summary

....
....
....
....
....
....
....
....
....

Best Characters & Why I Liked Them

....
....
....
....

My Thoughts

_____

_____

_____

_____

_____

_____

_____

_____

_____

_____

Best Quotes & Stand Out Moments

	Page

My Review . . .

Title: ....

Author: ....

Date: .... Rating: ☆☆☆☆☆

☐ Book ☐ Audiobook ☐ eBook

I would recommend this book to:

....

Summary

....
....
....
....
....
....
....
....
....
....
....

Best Characters & Why I Liked Them

....
....
....
....

My Thoughts

Best Quotes & Stand Out Moments

	Page

My Review . . .

Title: ....

Author: ....

Date: .... Rating: ☆☆☆☆☆

☐ Book ☐ Audiobook ☐ eBook

I would recommend this book to:

....

Summary

....
....
....
....
....
....
....
....
....

Best Characters & Why I Liked Them

....
....
....
....

My Thoughts

Best Quotes & Stand Out Moments

	Page

Books To Read

Books To Read . . .

Title	Author	Read
		☐
		☐
		☐
		☐
		☐
		☐
		☐
		☐
		☐
		☐
		☐
		☐
		☐
		☐
		☐
		☐

Title	Author	Read
		☐
		☐
		☐
		☐
		☐
		☐
		☐
		☐
		☐
		☐
		☐
		☐
		☐
		☐
		☐
		☐

Books To Read . . .

Title	Author	Read
		☐
		☐
		☐
		☐
		☐
		☐
		☐
		☐
		☐
		☐
		☐
		☐
		☐
		☐
		☐
		☐

Title	Author	Read
		☐
		☐
		☐
		☐
		☐
		☐
		☐
		☐
		☐
		☐
		☐
		☐
		☐
		☐
		☐
		☐

Notes

Notes . . .

Notes . . .

Notes . . .

Notes . . .

THE READING LOG

Let's Get Organised collection, first published by **FROM YOU TO ME LTD** in September 2024

For a full range of all our titles where gifts can also be personalised, please visit

WWW.FROMYOUTOME.COM

FROM YOU TO ME are committed to a sustainable future for our business, our customers and our planet. This book is printed and bound in China on FSC®certified paper.

1 3 5 7 9 11 13 15 14 12 10 8 6 4 2

ISBN 978-1-907048-74-6

FROM YOU TO ME LTD, STUDIO 100, THE OLD LEATHER FACTORY
GLOVE FACTORY STUDIOS, HOLT, WILTSHIRE, BA14 6RJ

I SBN 978-1-907048-74-6

9 781907 048746